Parrots

Published by Wildlife Education, Ltd.
9820 Willow Creek Road, Suite 300, San Diego, California 92131

ISBN 0-937934-84-4

Parrots

Created and Written by
John Bonnett Wexo

Zoological Consultant
Charles R. Schroeder, D.V.M.
Director Emeritus
San Diego Zoo and San Diego Wild Animal Park

Scientific Consultants
James Dolan, Ph.D.
General Curator
San Diego Zoo and San Diego Wild Animal Park

Kenton C. Lint
Curator of Birds Emeritus
San Diego Zoo

Art Credits

Pages Eight and Nine: Trevor Boyer

Pages Ten and Eleven: Trevor Boyer

Page Ten: Bottom Left, Raul Espinoza

Pages Twelve and Thirteen: Trevor Boyer

Page Twelve: Bottom Left, Walter Stuart

Page Thirteen: Top, Center and Bottom, Walter Stuart

Pages Sixteen and Seventeen: Trevor Boyer

Page Sixteen: Bottom Left, Walter Stuart

Pages Eighteen and Nineteen: Barbara Hoopes

Pages Twenty and Twenty-one: Barbara Hoopes

Page Twenty: Top, Middle and Bottom, Walter Stuart

Page Twenty-one: Top, Middle, Bottom Left and Right, Walter Stuart

Photographic Credits

Cover: Hans Reinhard *(Bruce Coleman, Inc.)*

Page Thirteen: Left, George Bryce *(Animals Animals);* **Middle,** Kenneth Fink *(Ardea London);* **Right,** Kenneth Fink *(Ardea London)*

Pages Fourteen and Fifteen: Jane Burton *(Bruce Coleman, Inc.)*

Page Sixteen: Top, G. C. Kelley *(Photo Researchers);* **Middle,** Academy of Natural Sciences of Philadelphia/*Vireo;* **Bottom,** L. Naylor *(Photo Researchers)*

Page Seventeen: Top, T. Parke *(Vireo);* **Middle,** David S. Rimlinger; **Bottom,** G. Ziesler *(Peter Arnold, Inc.)*

Page Eighteen: Top, Stephen Krasemann *(DRK Photo);* **Middle,** Stephen Krasemann *(DRK Photo);* **Bottom,** Hans Reinhard *(Bruce Coleman, Inc.)*

Page Nineteen: Top, Bob Campbell *(Bruce Coleman, Inc.);* **Middle,** Alan Weaving *(Ardea London);* **Bottom Left,** Jane Burton *(Bruce Coleman, Inc.);* **Bottom Right,** Hans Reinhard *(Bruce Coleman, Inc.)*

Page Twenty: Top, Stephen Krasemann *(DRK Photo);* **Middle,** Stephen Krasemann *(DRK Photo);* **Bottom,** Hans Reinhard *(Bruce Coleman, Inc.)*

Page Twenty-one: Top, Bob Campbell *(Bruce Coleman, Inc.);* **Middle,** Alan Weaving *(Ardea London);* **Bottom Left,** Jane Burton *(Bruce Coleman, Inc.);* **Bottom Right,** Hans Reinhard *(Bruce Coleman, Inc.)*

Page Twenty-two and Twenty-three: Fritz Prenzel *(Animals Animals)*

Our Thanks To: Bill Knerr *(San Diego Zoo Propagator);* Ed Hamilton *(San Diego Bionomics Consultant);* Amadeo Rea and David Faulkner *(San Diego Museum of Natural History);* Don Patten *(Los Angeles County Museum);* Kimball Garrett *(Los Angeles County Museum);* Mrs. Reynolds *(San Diego Public Library);* Michaele Robinson and Janet Lombard *(San Diego Zoo Library);* Dr. Art Risser *(San Diego Zoo).*

Cover Photo: Red-lored parrot

Contents

Parrots are very popular with people, for several obvious reasons. To begin with, they are beautiful. Many parrot species are covered from head to tail with brilliantly colored feathers. And many of them have other ornaments, such as crests, that add to their beauty. There are only a few other groups of birds in the world that can match the splendor of the parrots.

People are also impressed and charmed by the ability that some parrots have to "talk." In some cases, this ability seems truly astounding. The African Gray parrot, for example, can be taught to mimic men, women, children, and other animals. There have been parrots that could recite speeches, or tell a whole string of jokes. At times, parrots can be so good at saying words and phrases that we are almost convinced that they know what they are saying.

But, of course, they don't really understand any of it. They are just good "copycats," with an excellent knack for imitating the sounds they hear. There is a mystery to this, all the same. It seems that wild parrots in the jungle don't imitate the sounds of other birds and animals. Among captive parrots, the African Gray parrot is the best "talker."

The "talking" of parrots appeals to us because it seems so similar to our own behavior. And parrots do other things that are appealing for the same reason. For instance, they are usually very loyal to their mates. Many times, the "husband" and "wife" in a mated pair of parrots stay together for life. They are good parents, too. While most bird parents push their young out of the nest as soon as possible, parrots may allow their young to stay around (and be fed) for a long time.

With most parrot species, it is easy to tell the males and the females apart. Males usually have more colorful feathers, which they use to attract the females. However, in some parts of the world, female parrots and parakeets may be as brightly colored as the males — and this makes it almost impossible to tell them apart.

Some types of parrots can live a long time. Cockatoos in zoos have lived more than 70 years — and some people claim they can live even longer than that.

A flock of parrots in flight is one of nature's most beautiful sights. These are galah cockatoos from Australia.

The wonderful variety of parrots adds a rainbow of colors to the animal world. A few parrots have feathers that are dull brown or tan. But most of them are dressed in vivid reds, greens, yellows, and blues. There are over 300 different species, and some of the most beautiful are shown here.

GOLDEN CONURE
Aratinga guarouba

YELLOW-HEADED AMAZON
Amazona ochrocephala tresmariae

SCARLET MACAW
Ara macao

SULPHUR-CRESTED COCKATOO
Cacatua galerita

BUDGERIGAR
Melopsittacus undulatus

PALM COCKATOO
Probosciger atterimus

AFRICAN GRAY PARROT
Psittacus erithacus

LILAC-CROWN AMAZON
Amazona finschi

BLOSSOM-HEADED PARAKEET
Psittacula roseata

MASCARENE PARROT
Macarinus mascarinus (Extinct)

EASTERN ROSELLA
Platycercus eximius

COCKATIEL
Nymphicus hollandicus

8

GALAH
Eolophus roseicapillus

HAWK-HEADED PARROT
Deroptyus accipitrinus

ST. VINCENT'S AMAZON
Amazona guildingii

GREAT-BILLED PARROTS
Tanygnathus megalorynchos

ULTRAMARINE LORY
Vini ultramarina

KEA
Nestor notabilis

WHITE-NAPED LORY
Lorius albidinuchus

HYACINTH MACAW
Anodorynchus hyacinthinus

BLUE-CROWNED RACKET-TAILED
PARROT
Prioniturus discurus platenae

BUFFON'S MACAW
Ara ambigua

PESQUET'S PARROT
Psittrichas fulgidus

BUFF-FACED PYGMY PARROT
Micropsitta pusio

PAINTED CONURE
Pyrrhura picta

KAKAPO
Strigops habroptilus

BLUE-AND-GOLD MACAW
Ara ararauna

MASKED LOVEBIRD
Agapornis personata

9

A parrot's body is made for living in a tropical forest. In such a place, there are many brightly colored leaves, flowers and fruits. So the bright colors of the birds actually help them to hide from predators. When a parrot perches on a branch high up in a tree, it may look like a piece of fruit or a flower. Parrots get most of their food from trees, by gathering seeds, nuts and fruits. And their bodies are specially designed for this, as you will see on these pages.

For a bird, a parrot has a rather plump body. So it must have strong muscles in its legs and wings in order to fly, or even to climb around in the trees.

The feathers of parrots are like flags. Every parrot species in the world has its own special colors, just as every country in the world has its own flag. Each parrot can tell if another parrot is a member of the same species by looking at the colors it is wearing.

The feet of parrots have an unusually strong grip. Each foot has four long toes. Two of the toes point forward and two point backward. This arrangement makes it easy for them to grab slippery seeds, nuts, or fruit. And they can grab a branch so tightly that they can hang upside down, if they want to. Or they can stand on one foot when they eat.

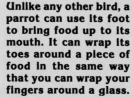

Unlike any other bird, a parrot can use its foot to bring food up to its mouth. It can wrap its toes around a piece of food in the same way that you can wrap your fingers around a glass.

Like all flying birds, parrots have many bones that are hollow. This helps to make their bodies lighter, so it is easier for them to fly. But even with hollow bones, parrots are heavier than most birds. So they have to flap their wings very fast to stay up in the air.

All parrots have hooked bills, and this is really the easiest way to see if a bird is a parrot. But there is a great deal of variety in the shapes of the hooks. This is because different kinds of parrots need different types of hooks for eating different kinds of foods.

SLENDER-BILLED CORELLA

A few parrots dig up roots and bulbs from the ground. The upper part of their bills is long, so they can use the bills like shovels.

RED-CAPPED PARROT

Some parrots use their bills to scrape seeds out of pods. For this reason, their bills are pointed and very sharp, like paring knives.

PALM COCKATOO

This bird likes to eat nuts that have hard shells. It has a big, thick bill that can crush even the toughest nut.

LORY

Lories don't dig, scrape, or crack anything. They get most of their food by drinking nectar and eating pollen from flowers. So their bills are small and weak.

11

Different kinds of parrots have so many different kinds of names that it may seem confusing. But all parrots belong to only three main groups: (1) the *parrots and parakeets*, (2) the *lories and lorikeets*, and (3) the *cockatoos*.

The parrots and parakeet group is the largest. It includes the biggest parrots, called *macaws*, and the smallest, called *pygmy parrots*. Among the other members of the group are the *conures* (CON-YERZ), *keas* (KEY-UZ), and *amazons*.

On these pages, we've shown you some of the major types of parrots—and some of the ways you can tell one from another.

GREEN-WINGED MACAW

Many kinds of parrots have a small ring of skin around each of their eyes, like the amazon at left. But only macaws have large patches of skin on the sides of their faces.

IMPERIAL AMAZON

PURPLE-BELLIED LORY

Lories have remarkable tongues for collecting nectar and pollen from flowers. The tongue looks like a tiny brush with hundreds of little bristles. The lory can poke its tongue into a flower and brush up the nectar and pollen.

Ⓐ

Ⓒ

The tails of parrots come in many shapes and sizes. They may be short and square, like an amazon parrot's tail Ⓐ. Or long and pointed, like a parakeet's Ⓑ. The tails of racket-tailed parrots are really strange. There are two feathers in the middle that look like long tennis rackets Ⓒ, but the rest of the tail is short and square.

The red areas on this map show where parrots live. As you can see, most of them live in warm parts of the world. But a few are found in places where you'd never expect to find them.

Slaty-headed parakeets live farther north than any other parrot species. They are found in the mountains of Afghanistan ①.

The Kea of New Zealand ③ likes the cold so much that it rolls around in the snow.

The tip of South America has some of the worst weather in the world. But Austral conures still live there ②.

KEA

AUSTRAL CONURE ②

①

③

GOLDEN-MANTLED RACKET-TAIL PARROT

LONG-TAILED PARAKEET

Most cockatoos carry a crest of pointed feathers on top of their heads. They can raise or lower the crests whenever they want to.

RED-BREASTED PYGMY PARROT

B

Pygmy parrots have sharp spines on the tips of their tails. The tips dig into the bark of a tree and hold the parrot steady while it looks for insects to eat.

MAJOR MITCHELL'S COCKATOO

Like many parrots, these Blue and Gold Macaws spend a lot of their time fighting with each other.

Families are important in the lives of parrots. Father and mother parrots work as a team to hatch their eggs and care for their young.

As you can see at right, the family nest is usually very simple. Most parrots just find a big hole in a tree. And most of the time, the eggs are simply laid on the dust and dead wood that was already in the hole. However, there are some parrots that nest in different ways, as you will see below.

ORANGE-FRONTED PARAKEETS

In dry places, where there aren't many trees, parrots may build their nests in cactus plants.

KEA

A few species build nests on the ground. They sometimes use holes or cracks in rocks to shelter the nests.

Baby parrots are born naked, except for a thin covering of down on their backs. Their eyes don't open until they are nearly two weeks old. And they are almost helpless for the first month of their lives. After the babies hatch, the mother stays with them, while the father goes out to get food.

There are even parrots that dig nest holes in termite mounds. The termites don't seem to bother the parrots.

MONK PARAKEETS

16

Most parrot nests are only large enough for a single family. But Monk parakeets build huge nests of grass that can be big enough for many families. The nests are like apartment houses, with separate "rooms" for each family.

This tiny chick is about 3 weeks old. Its first real feathers are just beginning to grow. At this stage, the feathers look like pins, so they are called *pinfeathers*.

Parrot eggs look a lot like chicken eggs. They are round, and almost pure white. After the eggs are laid, the mother and father take turns sitting on them —although the mother usually does more sitting than the father. It takes about 3 weeks for the eggs of most parrots to hatch.

Only a few types of parrots gather twigs and leaves to line their nests. And hanging parrots have a very strange way of carrying these things back to the nest. They stuff everything into their tail feathers, so it won't get in the way when they fly. This makes the parrots looks like flying pincushions.

MACAW

Most kinds of parrots are very sociable. They like to gather in large flocks. And there may be more than a thousand parrots in a single flock.

Male and female parrots almost always live together in pairs. Some parrots, like the lovebirds at right, show an almost human affection for each other. They like to sit together, rubbing their bills together and preening each other's feathers.

Wouldn't it be wonderful to have a wild parrot for a pet? Or some other wild animal? Just think how your friends would envy you, and how much fun it would be.

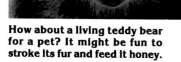

How about a living teddy bear for a pet? It might be fun to stroke its fur and feed it honey.

Why wait for the circus to come to town? Your own elephant will give you a ride whenever you like—and maybe help you wash the car!

Why settle for a goldfish or a hamster, when you could have a pair of beautiful fig parrots instead?

Have you ever seen anything that looks as cute and cuddly as a bushbaby?

If you have an extra swimming pool, a friendly alligator is just the thing for you. One thing is certain—you'll be the only person on your block that has one.

Your friends will really think you're rich if you own a macaw. Some of these beautiful birds cost more than $5,000.

You'll always have something to talk to when you've got a pair of cockatoos.

Wild parrots belong in the wild.

And so do all other wild animals. It might be fun to think about, but actually *owning* a wild animal would be very difficult. And no matter how hard you might try, you could never make it as happy as it would be in the wild.

A full-grown bear with great big claws can be hard on your furniture.

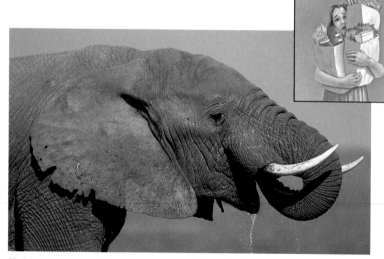

Unless you're a millionaire, you could go broke trying to buy an elephant enough food to eat.

Wild animals can make an awful mess. These parrots like to spread seeds and other foods all over the place.

Bushbabies are night animals. When you want to sleep, they want to play.

You never know when an alligator might suddenly get hungry.

Cockatoos like to start shrieking very early in the morning. They'll get you up every day at the crack of dawn.

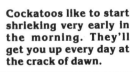

Macaws like to crack things open with their big, strong beaks.

Wild parrots are in danger today.
People are capturing too many of them to sell as pets. And the forests they live in are being chopped down, so people can build farms or sell the wood.

Something must be done now to stop the destruction of the forests and the trapping of birds, or there will soon be no more beautiful wild parrots. There is one thing we can all do to help. We can refuse to buy parrots that have been taken from the wild. And we can ask our friends to do the same.

RAINBOW LORIES

23

Index